Sea Turtle Night

Written by Kana Riley

The sun goes down. Day turns to night.
Terns fly home to their nests.

3

A mother sea turtle walks out of the water.
She walks with slow, sure steps.

4

She turns left. She turns right. When she finds
a good spot, she digs a hole.

She lays many round white eggs.

She covers the eggs with sand. She wants to make sure nothing can hurt them.

Then the mother turtle turns away. With slow, sure steps, she returns to the water.

She will not see the eggs hatch. She will never see the little turtles.

9

The sun comes up. Night turns to day. The terns fly over the beach. They cannot see the turtle eggs in the sand.

Many days and many nights pass. Little turtles burst out of their shells. But they stay in the sand until it is night.

Then the little turtles hurry across the sand.

12

They hurry to the water. No one has to teach them what to do.

The sun comes up. Night turns to day.
The terns fly over the beach.

They see a pile of sand where the turtle eggs used to be.

The little turtles have gone to live in the water.